NATURE WATCH
GREAT APES

Barbara Taylor
Consultant: Ian Redmond,
Chairman, Ape Alliance (www.4apes.com)

LORENZ BOOKS

C O N

First published in 2001 by Lorenz Books

© Anness Publishing Limited 2001

Lorenz Books is an imprint of Anness Publishing Limited, Hermes House, 88–89 Blackfriars Road, London SE1 8HA. www.lorenzbooks.com

Published in the USA by Lorenz Books, Anness Publishing Inc., 27 West 20th Street, New York, NY 10011; (800) 554–9657.

This edition distributed in Canada by Raincoast Books, 8680 Cambie Street, Vancouver, British Columbia, V6P 6M9.

A CIP catalogue record for this book is available from the British Library

Publisher: Joanna Lorenz
Managing Editor, Children's Books: Gilly Cameron Cooper
Senior Editor: Nicole Pearson
Editor: Jennifer Davidson
Designer: Ann Samuel
Picture Researcher: Wendy Wilders
Illustrators: Julian Baker, Vanessa Card, David Webb
Production Controller: Yolande Denny
Editorial Reader: Jonathan Marshall

10 9 8 7 6 5 4 3 2 1

PICTURE CREDITS
b=bottom, t=top, c= centre, l= left, r= right

ABPL: Martin Harvey: 28bl, 34bl, 43tr, 43br, 61tr/Anup Shah: 6tl, 18bl. AKG photo: 5t, 25tr. Heather Angel: 17tl. BBC Natural History Unit: Karen Bass: 2b, 40tl/Bruce Davidson: 23tl, 25tl, 26tr, 57tr/Ian Redmond: 59tr Michael W Richards 9tr/Anup Shah: 15bl, 17bl, 24tr, 35cl, 38tl, 49c, Tom Vezo: 6bl, 64b. Bob Campbell: 16tr. Bruce Coleman: Ingo Arndt: 22tl/R I M Campbell: 5tl, 11tl/Alain Compost: 39br, 44bl/Gerald S Cubitt: 9tl, 59br/Peter Davey: 1c, 28tl/Steven C Kaufman: 55tr/Mary Plage: 9b/Jorg and Petra Wegner: 7br, 20, 65b/Rod Williams: 25bl, 51br, 55tl, 55tl/Gunter Ziesler: 14bl. e. t. archive, 55br. FLPA: Frank W Lane: 31cr. M Harvey: 10tl. The Kobal Collection: 5cr, 7bl, 18br, 27br, 57br. Mary Evans Picture Library: 51bl. Oxford Scientific Films: Bob Bennett: 15br/Joe Blossom: 47tl, 52b/Clive Bromhall: 3b, 18tr, 29br, 29tl, 32br, 35tl, 35br, 37bl, 38tl, 47tr, 50tl, 56b, 63t/Martyn Colbeck: 7tl, 40br, 41tr/E R Degginger: 21tr, 21cl/Michael Dick: 59tl/Jackie Le Fevre: 15bl, 36b/Nick Gordon: 49tr/David Haring: 55cl/Mike Hill: 45br/Michael Leach: 15tr/Joe Mcdonald: 33tl/Stan Osolinski: 32bl/Andrew Plumptre: 5tr, 9cr, 10br, 11tr, 23br, 30tl, 39tr, 39bl, 42t/Ralph Reinhold: 19br/Steve Turner: 34tl/Konrad Wothe: 2tl, 2tr, 11bl, 14tl, 17tr, 31c, 45tl, 45bl. NASA: 57tl. NHPA: G I Bernard: 59cl/Joe Blossom: 43bl/Mark Bowler: 46l/Steven Dalton: 52tl/Nigel J Dennis: 25br, 43tl, 53t/Jeff Goodman: 36tl Martin Harvey: 6br, 17br, 37tl, 48b, 59tl, 61tl, 61cl, 61br/Daniel Heuclin: 41bl, 41tl, 60b/Gerard Lacz: 56tr/Michael Leach: 5br, 62b. Haroldo Palo Jnr: 55bl/Christophe Ratier 10bl, 35br/Steve Robinson: 28br, 33bl, 35tr, 35bl 46r/Kevin Schaffer: 54t. Papilio Photographic: 24br, 49tl. Photo Researchers Incorporated: 29tr. Planet Earth: K & K Ammann: 11bl, 27tl, 30b, 31br, 33tr, 41br, 58b/Andre Baertschi: 15br/Tom Brakefield: 45tr/John Downer: 57tr/Brian Kenney: 15tl, 62t/Ken Lucas: 21cr, 55br/Jonathan P Scott 47bl/Anup Shah: 4bl, 8t, 22br, 23cl, 24bl, 44br/Denise Tackett: 54b. Ian Redmond: 42b, 47br, 48tl, 58t. Tony Stone: Howie Garber: 49bl/Renee Lynn: 19tl. Georgia State University: Anna Clopet: 27bl, 27tr. Warner Bros: 60tl. WSPA: 57bl.

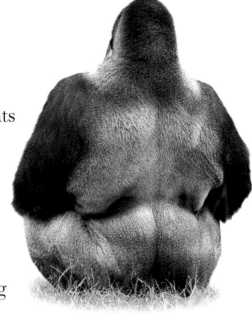

TENTS

What is a Great Ape?

The four great apes—the chimpanzee, bonobo, gorilla, and orangutan—look similar to us because they are our closest animal relatives. Humans are sometimes called the fifth great ape. The great apes are also closely related to the lesser apes, the gibbons. Nearly 99 percent of our genes are the same as those of a chimpanzee, in fact, chimpanzees are more closely related to humans than they are to gorillas. Like us, the other great apes are intelligent, use tools, solve problems, and communicate. They can also learn a language, although their vocal cords cannot produce the right range of sounds to speak.

▼ **APE FEATURES**
Gorillas are the largest of the great apes. Typical ape features include long arms (longer than their legs), flexible wrist joints, gripping thumbs and fingers, and no tail. Apes are clever, with big brains.

▲ **RED APE**
Red, shaggy orangutans are the largest tree-living animals in the world. Their name means person-of-the-forest. Orangutans live on the islands of Borneo and Sumatra in Southeast Asia.

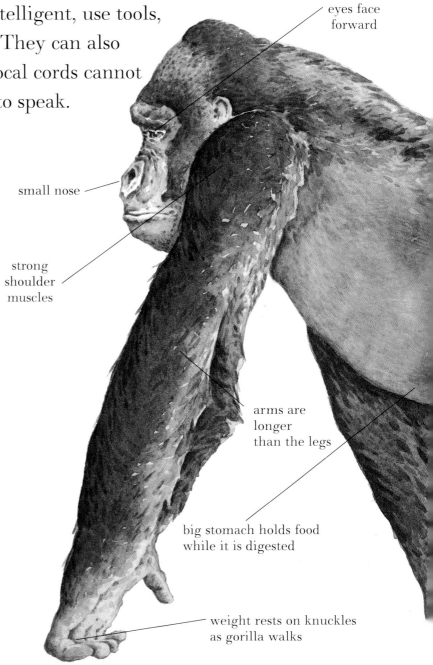

eyes face forward

small nose

strong shoulder muscles

arms are longer than the legs

big stomach holds food while it is digested

weight rests on knuckles as gorilla walks

4

GROUPS ▶
Family groups of between five and 40 gorillas live together in the misty rain forests and mountains of Central Africa. Each group is led by an adult male. He decides where the group will feed, sleep, and travel.

▲ **STUDYING APES**
Much of what we know today about wild apes is based on the work of scientists such as Dr. Dian Fossey, who spent many years carefully observing gorillas in the wild.

apes do not have a tail

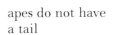

King Kong
At the beginning of the 1930s, the film King Kong *showed a giant gorilla as a dangerous monster. In the movie, a team of hunters capture Kong and take him to America. We now know that gorillas are peaceful animals, very different from the movie monster.*

feet rest flat on the ground

▼ **APE FACES**
Have you ever watched a chimpanzee in a zoo and found that it has turned to watch you? Great apes are often as interested in watching us, as we are in watching them.

Ape Shapes and Sizes

It's hard to believe that a tiny newborn gorilla, half the weight of most human babies, may grow up to be a heavyweight male that weighs almost 440 pounds. Gorillas are the largest of the four great apes, while chimpanzees and bonobos are the smallest—similar in size to a 12-year-old boy or girl. Male great apes are up to twice the size and weight of females. This helps them to frighten predators and rivals. However, male and female gibbons are the same size. They are much smaller than the great apes, and so are known as the lesser apes. Their small size allows them to live high in the trees all the time. Large male gorillas are too heavy for a permanent treetop lifestyle, although they do climb trees for fruit and buds.

▲ **SMALL APE**
Male chimpanzees stand just under five feet tall and weigh up to 88 pounds. Females are a little shorter and lighter. Chimpanzees have muscular bodies and are strong for their size.

orangutan
(Pongo pygmaeus)

◄ **BIG FACE**
A fully grown male orangutan has fatty pads the size of dinner plates on his cheeks. They make him look bigger and help him to frighten off rival males.

▲ **SIZE DIFFERENCE**
Male gorillas are twice the size of females. A wild male gorilla stands about six feet tall and is incredibly muscular. A female gorilla is shorter—about five feet—and weighs 198 pounds.

bonobo or pygmy chimpanzee
(Pan paniscus)

◄ **A NEW SPECIES**

Bonobos used to be known as pygmy chimpanzees, but they were recognized as a separate species in 1929. Bonobos are about the same height as chimpanzees at the shoulder, but they have a more slender and leggy body. Bonobos also have smaller, rounder heads compared to chimpanzees. The hair on a bonobo's head usually looks like it has been parted in the middle.

Did you know? A big male orangutan is the weight of a heavyweight boxer.

► **LESSER APE**

The gibbons are the smallest and lightest of the apes. Most gibbons measure just over 24 inches in length and weigh less than 15 pounds. There are 11 species of gibbon. The heaviest species is the siamang— the males weigh up to 31 pounds.

white-cheeked gibbon
(Hylobates concolor leucogenys)

Yeti and Bigfoot

Some people believe that an apeman lives hidden in the high mountains of Asia and the wilderness areas of North America. It is called the Yeti or the Abominable Snowman in the Himalayas and Bigfoot or Sasquatch in North America.

Ape Habitats

If you want to see wild apes in their natural habitats, you have to travel to tropical Africa or Southeast Asia. Most apes live in tropical rain forests, but some chimpanzees are found in more open, deciduous woodlands or in wooded grasslands, and some gorillas prefer mountain forests, with their lush vegetation and misty atmosphere. In some places, gibbons live in deciduous forests, too. All the apes used to be more widespread, but over time, they are being gradually squeezed into smaller and smaller areas, as people have hunted them and destroyed their habitats.

▲ VANISHING APE
In the dark and dappled rain forest where orangutans live, their shaggy, orange hair blends in with the tangle of forest plants. This makes them surprisingly difficult to see.

GORILLA SIGNS ▶
It is often hard for scientists to watch gorillas in their forest habitats. Instead, the scientists study the signs left behind by the gorillas as they move around.

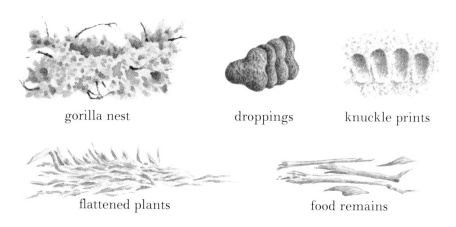

gorilla nest   droppings   knuckle prints

flattened plants   food remains

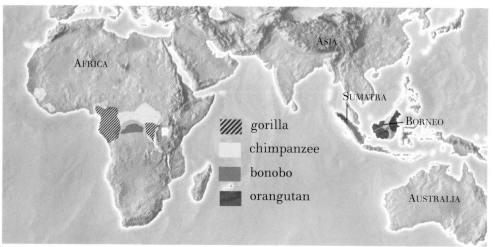

◀ WHERE APES LIVE
Gorillas, chimpanzees, and bonobos live in Africa, and orangutans live only on the islands of Borneo and Sumatra. However, orangutans once lived in parts of mainland Southeast Asia. Some people believe that they were hunted out by poachers.

ASIA
AFRICA
SUMATRA
BORNEO
AUSTRALIA

gorilla
chimpanzee
bonobo
orangutan

▲ ROUTE MAP

Chimpanzees travel around their own neighborhoods on the ground, following a network of paths. They use a mental map in their heads to decide where to go. Each day they figure out where to get a good meal, climbing trees to find fruit and leaves, or to chase prey.

▲ TREETOP APE

Gibbons are totally at home in the tops of the trees and hardly ever go down to the ground. They are the only apes that do not build nests. They sleep sitting up in the forks of branches, resting on tough sitting pads. These pads act like built-in cushions.

▲ MOUNTAIN HOME

Mountain gorillas live in dense, misty forests up to about 11,500 feet above sea level. At night, the temperature may drop to below freezing, but the long hair of the mountain gorillas helps them to keep warm.

▼ NIGHT NESTS

Every night, the adult great apes make nests in the trees or on the ground. They bend and weave together leafy branches, and pile more leaves and branches on top. This makes a warm, springy nest to keep out the cold.

chimpanzee
(Pan troglodytes)

Focus on

It's 6:30 in the morning. A group of gorillas is waking up. They are hungry after their night-time fast and reach out to pick a leafy breakfast in bed. Then the gorillas move on through the forest, feeding as they go. After a morning spent munching plants, they build day nests on the ground and rest for a couple of hours. This gives them time to digest their food and socialize. They are mountain gorillas. They live amid the beautiful and misty volcanic Virunga Mountains in Africa. They have lowland cousins who live in the tropical rain forests of eastern and western Central Africa.

CAREFUL CLIMBERS
Gorillas climb with great care and feel most secure when all four limbs are in contact with a branch. Young gorillas are lighter, and often play by hanging beneath branches and swinging like a gibbon.

MOUNTAIN REFUGE
In 1925, the home of the mountain gorillas on the slopes of the Virunga volcanoes was declared Africa's first national park. The word *virunga* comes from a local expression meaning isolated mountains that reach the clouds. The Virunga mountains include both active and dormant volcanoes, but the gorillas live only on the dormant volcanoes.

LOWLAND GORILLAS
Traveling through the Odzala Forest, these western lowland gorillas feed in a swampy glade. Like all gorillas, they walk on all fours.

Gorilla Habitats

GORILLA CHAMPION

From her hut on Mount Visoke, Dian Fossey devoted herself to studying and protecting mountain gorillas. She began her work in 1967, winning the trust of the gorillas, studying their family relationships, and making discoveries about their behavior.

CLOUD FORESTS

Mists often swirl around the forests where the mountain gorillas live, so they are called cloud forests. Mosses and lichens grow well in the cool, damp air, and hang on the branches like untidy green hair.

LOWLAND FORESTS

Eastern lowland gorillas live in the dense lowland rain forests of eastern Congo. These forests are less open than the mountain gorillas' habitat, so it is more difficult for people to study lowland gorillas.

FOOD FOR FREE

On the rainy slopes where they live, the mountain gorillas have a wide variety of food, such as wild celery, bedstraw, bamboo shoots, thistles, brambles, and nettles.

Bodies and Bones

Characteristic features of great apes are their long, strong arms and flexible shoulders, which they use to clamber through the trees. They do not have tails to help them balance and grip the branches. Instead of hooves or paws, apes have hands and feet that can grasp branches and hold food very well. On the ground, an ape's strong arms and fingers take its weight as it walks on all fours. Humans are different from the other apes, because they have short arms and long legs. Human arms are about 30 percent shorter than human legs. Our bodies and bones are also designed for walking upright, rather than for swinging through the trees. All the apes have a large head, with a big skull inside, to protect an intelligent brain.

◄ **APE SKELETON**
One of the notable features of an ape skeleton is the large skull that surrounds and protects the big brain. Apes also have long, strong finger and toe bones for gripping. The arm bones of the orangutans, gorillas, and chimpanzees are also extended, making their arms longer than their legs.

Did you know? Female orangutans weigh up to 80 lbs, but males can weigh over 200 lbs.

▼ **THE BIG FIVE**
The five great apes have similar bodies, although a human's body is less hairy and muscular than the body of a great ape. The main differences between ape bodies lie in the shape of the skull and the length of the arms and legs. Orangutans have extra long arms to hang from branches, but humans have long legs for walking upright.

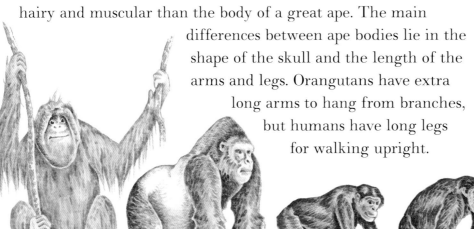

orangutan   gorilla   bonobo   chimpanzee   human

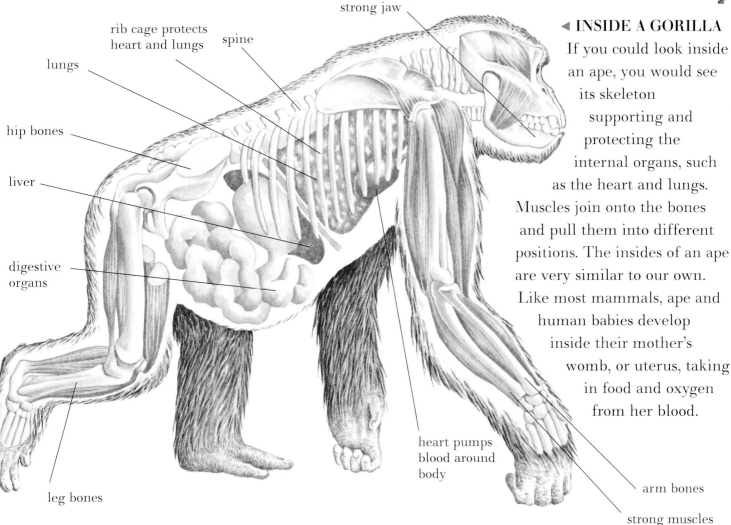

strong jaw

rib cage protects
heart and lungs
spine

lungs

hip bones

liver

digestive
organs

leg bones

heart pumps
blood around
body

arm bones

strong muscles

◀ **INSIDE A GORILLA**
If you could look inside
an ape, you would see
its skeleton
supporting and
protecting the
internal organs, such
as the heart and lungs.
Muscles join onto the bones
and pull them into different
positions. The insides of an ape
are very similar to our own.
Like most mammals, ape and
human babies develop
inside their mother's
womb, or uterus, taking
in food and oxygen
from her blood.

▲ **NO TAIL**
Apes such as this chimpanzee, do not
have tails, but most monkeys do. Apes
clamber and hang by their powerful
arms. Monkeys walk along branches on
all fours, using the tail for balance.

EXTRA HAND ▶
Many of the
monkeys that live
in the dense
rain forests of
Central and South
America have
special gripping
tails, called
prehensile tails.
The tails also have
sensitive tips that
work like an extra
one-fingered
hand, allowing
them to cling to
the branches when
they gather fruit.

13

western lowland gorilla
(Gorilla gorilla gorilla)

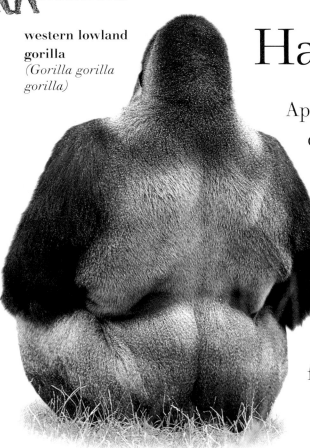

▲ **SILVER LEADER**
When a male gorilla is about 11 or 12 years old, he grows a saddle-shaped area of silvery gray hair on his back, and long, shaggy hair on his arms. He also loses his chest hair. He is called a silverback, and these changes show he is grown-up. Males whose hair has not yet changed are called blackbacks.

GROOMING ▶
Chimpanzees regularly search through each other's hair with their fingers, carefully picking out any dirt and lice, and cleaning cuts and scratches. Grooming feels pleasant, and it helps the apes to relax and reassure each other. It also helps to strengthen friendships.

Hairy Apes

Apes are mammals, like cats, bears, mice, and deer. Mammals are warm-blooded animals, and most have hair-covered bodies. The hair grows out of little pits in the skin called follicles, forming a layer that traps warm air given off by the body. This helps to keep an ape warm. Apes that live in colder places, such as mountain gorillas, have longer, thicker hair for extra warmth. Apes don't like the rain, because their hair is not very waterproof. Sometimes apes try to shelter from the rain or make umbrellas out of large leaves, but often they just sit hunched up, waiting for the rain to stop. Male and female chimpanzees both have black hair, and all orangutans have orange-red coats, but adult male gorillas have a distinctive silver back, and some male and female gibbons are totally different colors.

◄ **COLOR CONTRAST**

In some species of gibbon, males and females have different colored hair. For instance, male concolor and hoolock gibbons are black, and females are a golden color. Male and female lar gibbons are the same color, but populations living in different places may be different colors.

▲ **TURNING GRAY**

Chimpanzees can live for 40 or 50 years. As a chimpanzee grows older, its coat fades and may turn gray. Its hair also thins, and older chimps may start to go bald.

white-handed gibbons
(Hylobates lar)

orangutan
(Pongo pygmaeus)

LONG HAIR ►

Orangutans from Sumatra have longer, thicker hair than those from Borneo. Scientists now think that they are a separate species from their Bornean relatives. Sumatran males have shaggy faces, with long, rich beards and moustaches that extend out onto their cheeks. Even female Sumatran orangutans have impressive chin hair. The long hair of male orangutans makes them look bigger and helps to scare off their rivals.

▲ **HAIRY SIGNALS**

This chimpanzee has made its hair stand on end to make itself look bigger and more frightening. A nervous or fearful chimp has flattened hair and a "fear grin."

Hands and Feet

Can you imagine how difficult it would be to pick something up if your arms ended in paws, hooves, or flippers? It would be impossible to grip the object, and you could not turn it around, carry it, throw it, pull it apart, or put it together. An ape's hands and feet are remarkable. They are very adaptable, and the opposing thumb or big toe enables them to grasp firmly or hold delicately. Ape hands and feet are strong and flexible, allowing apes to climb, swing, and jump through the treetops. They also allow apes to reach food, investigate their surroundings, build nests, and groom their family and friends. With most apes, the feet look a lot like hands, but with humans, the feet look different, because human feet are adapted for walking rather than climbing.

▲ SMILE, PLEASE
Grasping a delicate camera lens, a gorilla demonstrates how it can pick up fragile objects without breaking them. A gorilla has thicker, sturdier hands than a person, with fingers the size of bananas and a smaller thumb. Its hands have to be strong so that they can support the weight of the gorilla's body when it walks around on all fours.

hands

orangutan   bonobo   chimpanzee   gorilla   human

feet

◄ LOOK-ALIKE HANDS
The hands of the great apes have several features in common, such as nails and long, sensitive fingers. The thumb on a great ape's hand turns at an angle and can press against each finger. The big toe on an ape's foot can also do this, except in humans. Bonobos have a unique feature not shared by the other apes—webbing between the second and third toes.

16

orangutan
(Pongo pygmaeus)

▲ **OPPOSABLE THUMB**

Since a great ape's thumb can easily touch, or oppose, its fingers, it is called an opposable thumb. This special thumb gives an ape's hand a precise pincer grip, allowing it to pick up objects as small as berries.

Did you know? Humans have over 5 million hairs on their bodies.

▲ **POWER GRIP**

An orangutan's arms and legs end in huge hands and feet that work like powerful clamps. Just one hand or foot can take the entire weight of the ape.

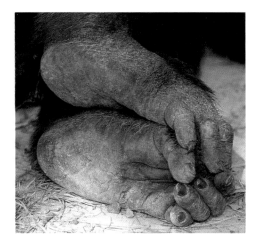

▲ **HAND-FOOT**

Unlike a human, a chimp can use its feet like hands, to hold and investigate things. The opposable big toe stretches out around one side of a branch, and the toes reach around the other side, forming a very strong grip.

▲ **FLAT FEET**

Chimpanzees are flat-footed, with tough, hairless feet and long toes. When they are upright, their feet must take all of the body weight.

Walking and Climbing

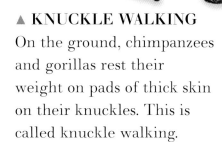

To an ape, the tangle of trunks, branches, and vines in a forest are like a gigantic climbing frame that provides high-level walkways through the air. Gibbons, orangutans, and bonobos spend a lot of time in the trees. Large male orangutans also travel on the ground some of the time, because of their great weight. The true masters of treetop travel are the gibbons, who are able to leap and swing effortlessly across gaps at high speed and at great heights. Chimpanzees and gorillas are mainly ground-based creatures, although chimpanzees are equally at home in the trees or on the ground. Gorillas, even with their bulk, are amazingly agile (if somewhat careful) climbers.

▲ **KNUCKLE WALKING**
On the ground, chimpanzees and gorillas rest their weight on pads of thick skin on their knuckles. This is called knuckle walking.

▲ **CLIMBING CHIMP**
Chimpanzees climb into the trees to find leaves or fruit to eat, to chase prey, and to build sleeping nests. Their long fingers hook over the branches and give them a good grip for both climbing and swinging.

Tarzan of the Apes
The American writer Edgar Rice Burroughs created the Tarzan character in a magazine story published in 1912. Tarzan was orphaned as a baby in the jungles of Africa. A tribe of great apes takes care of him, teaching him how to survive in the jungle and swing through trees. He shares his later adventures with his wife, Jane, and their son, Korak.

orangutans
(Pongo pygmaeus)

◀ **FLEXIBLE APE**

The body weight of an orangutan is evenly shared between its arms and legs. This helps the orangutan to keep its balance. The shoulder and hip joints of an orangutan are very supple, allowing it to stretch easily between branches. Orangutans can even eat hanging upside down. They can sway slender trees until they can reach far enough to catch a branch on the next tree. They often make a lot of noise crashing though the trees.

Did you know? A gorilla can run at 15–20 mph over short distances.

◀ **SWINGING GIBBONS**

With their amazingly long arms, gibbons swing at breathtaking speed from branch to branch, often leaping huge distances. Special wrist bones allow a gibbon to turn its body as it swings, without loosening its grip. This means it can swing hand-over-hand in a speedy swing, known as brachiating. Compared with the noisy crashings of monkeys leaping from tree to tree, gibbons are almost silent travelers.

▲ **GRIPPING FEAT**

Gorillas are wary tree climbers and rarely swing by their arms like chimps or gibbons. They climb down from a tree backward, holding the trunk loosely with both feet in a controlled slide.

19

Did you know? Gorilla skulls were used in ceremonies to give people the power of the gorilla.

Skulls and Teeth

An ape's skull is a hard casing of fused bones that surrounds and protects the large brain. The structure of the skull shows that an ape depends more on sight than smell as a way of gathering information about the outside world. The eyes are enclosed in bony sockets and are positioned on the front of the face. Since the sense of smell is less important, the face is flattened, with a smaller space for the nose. An ape's jaws are relatively well-developed, with 32 teeth—large, broad molars at the back, shovel-shaped incisors at the front for cutting, and pointed canines in between. The long canines can be used as weapons and when they are nervous, apes yawn to display them. In addition, chimpanzees sometimes make use of sticks and stones as weapons.

◀ **OPEN WIDE**
Gorillas have broad, flat molar teeth at the back of their mouths. These teeth grind, crush, and chew tough seeds and roots, such as nuts and wild ginger. Sharp, pointed canine teeth are used for tearing food. Males have large canine teeth that may be used for threat displays, or for fighting.

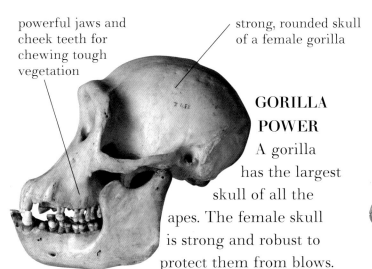

powerful jaws and cheek teeth for chewing tough vegetation

strong, rounded skull of a female gorilla

GORILLA POWER

A gorilla has the largest skull of all the apes. The female skull is strong and robust to protect them from blows. Male gorillas and some large females have bony ridges at the top of the skull, which are called sagittal crests. The big muscles that move the lower jaw are attached to this crest.

although chimpanzees eat meat, their teeth suggest that their ancestors' diet was mainly vegetarian

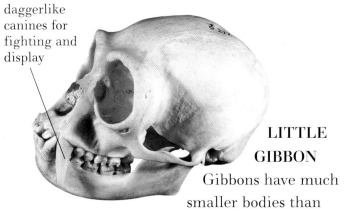

BRAINY CHIMP

Like a gorilla, a chimpanzee also has a strong jaw and protective bony ridges above the eyes. But its skull is thinner and not as robust as that of a gorilla. However, inside its skull, a chimpanzee has a much bigger brain than a gorilla, compared to its body size.

crushing cheek teeth, for grinding fruit and leaves

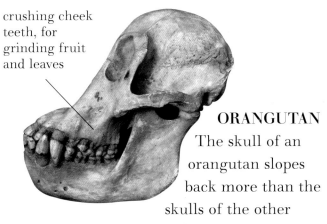

ORANGUTAN

The skull of an orangutan slopes back more than the skulls of the other great apes, and the bony ridges around the eye sockets are less developed. Like male gorillas, the big male orangutans have bony crests on the top of the skull for the attachment of large jaw muscles.

daggerlike canines for fighting and display

LITTLE GIBBON

Gibbons have much smaller bodies than the other apes, so their skulls are also smaller and more lightly built. There is little difference between the size of the skulls of male and female gibbons. A gibbon's skull is more rounded than those of the other apes.

Person-of-the-forest

In the Indonesian language, the meaning of orang *is person, and* hutan *means forest. Orangutans have inspired many myths. One is that orangutans were once humans exiled to the trees for displeasing the gods. Another is that they are descended from a man who ran away into the forest because he owed money.*

Food and Feeding

Apes feed mainly on fruit and leaves, but they also eat a small amount of animal food, such as insects. Chimpanzees have a more varied diet than the other apes, and occasionally eat red meat from birds and mammals, such as monkeys and young antelopes. Orangutans have also been seen eating young birds and squirrels. Apes spend a lot of time traveling around to find their food, which is spread out through the forest. If they stayed in one place, they would quickly use up all the food. They remember the locations of the best fruit trees in their area, and know when they will bear fruit. Apes have to eat a lot of food because their mainly plant food diet is often low in nutrients. As they cannot digest the tough fibers (cellulose) in the stems and leaves, much of what they eat passes through their gut undigested and out in their dung.

▲ HUNGRY GIBBON

Gibbons are mainly frugivores (feeding on fruit), but they also eat leaves and occasionally insects and eggs. They are so light that they can hang from thin branches and reach out their long arms to pick fruit growing right at the ends. Gibbons eat mainly ripe fruit.

FRUIT-EATERS ▶

Fruit forms about 65 percent of an orangutan's diet. The apes spread the seeds of fruit trees over a wide area by passing the seeds in their droppings far from the parent tree. This female has found a bunch of bananas, but another favorite food of the orangutan is durian tree fruit. The football-sized fruit contains a sweet-tasting, but foul-smelling flesh, which they adore. Orangutans also eat leaves, shoots, insects, and eggs.

▲ MASSIVE MEALS

Gorillas are mainly herbivores, munching their way through 44–66 pounds of greens per day. They eat with a lot of lip smacking and other noises of appreciation. Gorillas are careful eaters, often preparing their food by folding leaves into a wad or peeling off inedible layers. They drop unwanted parts, such as stalks, in a neat pile.

▲ HUNTING CHIMPS

Chimpanzees are clever predators, occasionally banding together in small groups to chase and catch animals such as monkeys, bush pigs, and small antelopes. A hunt can be long, lasting up to two hours, involving high-speed chases and ambushes, and causing great excitement.

▲ FOOD ALL AROUND

Mountain gorillas don't have to look very hard to find something to eat. Their plant food is all around them, so they just have to reach out a hand to pick a meal. Since they need to eat a lot of food, meals last two to four hours at a time. Gorilla days are mainly spent walking and eating food, then resting between meals to digest it. Their big stomach stores the food while it is being digested.

▼ CHIMP MEALS

Chimpanzees spend about six hours a day feeding, mostly just after sunrise and just before sunset. They eat a lot of fruit, which makes up about 68 percent of their diet, but they also eat leaves and other plant matter, and meat and insects.

chimpanzee
(Pan troglodytes)

Ape Senses

Apes are creatures of the daytime and their most important sense is their keen eyesight. Their forward-facing eyes can pick up fine detail, judge distances, and see in color. Their nose is a small, but useful, backup to the eyes. Their sense of smell is probably better than that of humans. Apes sniff food and each other, and also use their sense of smell to warn them of something unusual in their environment. If they do not recognize a smell, or if it makes them uneasy, they will use their eyes to investigate. The fact that apes rely more on sight than smell may be one reason why they have little hair on their faces. Facial expressions are easier to see without hair getting in the way, so they can be used as visual signals for communication.

▲ **EXCELLENT EYES**

The eyes of apes are set close together, facing forward. This enables both eyes to focus on the same object. The overlapping fields of vision allow three-dimensional sight for judging distance and depth accurately. This helps them to jump from branch to branch without falling.

◀ **NOSEPRINTS** ▶

Individual gorillas can be identified by the shape of their noses. The folds, wrinkles, and outline of a gorilla's nose are just as distinctive as its fingerprint. Each of the three subspecies of gorilla also has a different nose shape. These differences are especially clear when the nose of the mountain gorilla (left) is compared to that of a Western lowland gorilla (right).

▲ SENSITIVE SKIN

Like humans, gorillas have tiny raised ridges, or fingerprints, on the tips of their fingers. These ridges help gorillas feel and hold onto objects. Each gorilla's fingerprint is unique. Flat nails protect the sensitive fingertips from damage. A gorilla's hands respond to temperature and pressure, and also to touch.

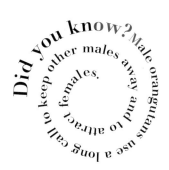

Did you know? Male orangutans use a long call to keep other males away and to attract females.

Three Wise Monkeys

A set of three Japanese monkeys were once used to explain Buddhist teachings. One monkey is covering its ears—this one represents the idea of hearing no evil. Another has its hands over its eyes so that it can see no evil. The third is stopping words from coming out of its mouth—representing the third wise saying of speak no evil.

NOISY APE ▶

Gibbons greatly rely on sound for communicating among the leafy treetops. When the siamang sings, its throat pouch swells up with air. This pouch of air acts like a resonating chamber to make its song even louder. Some other gibbons have these pouches, too, but not such big ones.

▼ SOUND SENSE

Big ears help chimpanzees to pick up the sounds drifting through the forest. They often stop and listen for the sounds of chimps or other animals, which may tell them of approaching danger. They also hoot to each other to keep in contact.

Smart Apes

Apes appear to be the brightest of all the nonhuman animals, but it is difficult to measure intelligence. Scientists think an intelligent animal is one that can solve problems, investigate and adapt to new conditions, behave in a flexible way, remember things, use tools, pass on information from one generation to the next, and even use language. Apes can do all these things, but their throats cannot make the sounds used by humans to produce a spoken language. Scientists have experimented with teaching apes signs and symbols in order to understand them better, and to investigate their intelligence. There is much debate about whether chimpanzees, bonobos, gorillas, or orangutans are the most intelligent of the great apes.

▲ **ESCAPE ARTISTS**
Captive orangutans are the master escapologists of the ape world. They use branches to ford deep moats full of water around their enclosures. They take out the center pins from hinges to open doors the wrong way, and they unravel chain-link fences.

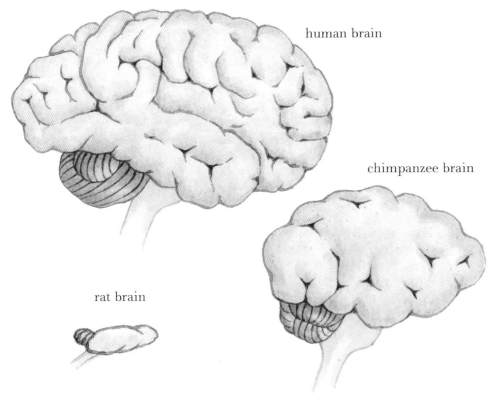

human brain

chimpanzee brain

rat brain

◄ **BRAIN POWER**
Humans and chimpanzees have much bigger brains than rats, even compared to body size. The bigger the brain, the less tied an animal is to set ways of doing things. Humans and chimps have large areas of the brain for learning, memory, reasoning, and judgment. This helps them to make decisions about what to do next, where to go, and what to eat.

▲ COMPUTER APE
At Yerkes Regional Primate Center near Atlanta, Georgia, bonobos and chimpanzees have been taught to communicate with a computer.

◄ APE ART
Many people have suggested that the way humans use art to express ideas is a measure of our intelligence. When captive apes have been allowed to experiment with pencils, paints, and paper, they have produced a variety of interesting images.

▲ HAND SPEAK
All four great apes have been taught sign language for simple communication. The apes have even taught fellow apes. Bonobos, such as Kanzi (above), have learned to communicate by pointing to specific symbols on a large board.

Planet of the Apes
In the film Planet of the Apes *(1968), three astronauts find themselves on a planet where apes are in control. Orangutans are judges and priests, chimpanzees are scholars, and gorillas are the police. Humans are hunted as stupid beasts. The hero realizes that this is an Earth of the future, where ape and human roles are reversed.*

Focus on

Humans were once thought to be the only animals smart enough to use tools. Now we know that a handful of other animals, such as Galapagos finches and sea otters, use them too. However, these animals are only beginners compared to chimpanzees. A chimp chooses its tools, changes them to make them better, and uses them over and over again. Chimps plan ahead, collecting sticks or stones on their way to a source of food. Their nimble fingers and creative minds help them to invent and use tools. Adult chimps are good at concentrating, sometimes spending hours using their tools.

USING A STICK

- This chimpanzee is shaping a stick to help her dig for food. Chimpanzees have invented clever ways to use sticks.

TASTY SNACKS

An intelligent chimp can shape and manipulate a grass stem to form a useful tool for fishing out termites from a mound. Scientists who have tried to copy the chimps have found that termite fishing is much, much harder than it looks.

SWEET AS HONEY

A captive chimp is using a stick, in the same way that a chimp in the wild would use a grass stem, to fish in a termite mound. However, the termite mound in the zoo probably has yogurt or honey inside it, instead of termites.

Chimp Tools

LEAF SPONGE

A wad of leaves makes a useful sponge to soak up rainwater from tree holes. Chewing the leaf first breaks up its waterproof coating, so it soaks up more water. Leaves may also be used as toilet paper, to wipe blood from wounds, and to scrape up sticky food.

STICK TOOLS

Wild chimps can only make tools from objects in their environment, which is why sticks are so important. Sticks make good weapons for attack and defense. They can also be used as levers, and thin sticks make a natural dental floss.

NUTCRACKERS

In West Africa, chimps use hammers and anvils to crack open the hard shells of nuts. Hammers are made from logs or stones, anvils from stones or tree roots. Hammer stones can weigh as much as 44 pounds. A skilled adult can crack a shell with just a few blows.

Living in a Group

Of all the apes, chimpanzees live in the largest groups—up to about 100 individuals. The chimps constantly change their friends and often drop out altogether to spend time on their own. A chimpanzee group is based around the most important male chimps, like gorilla groups, in which one of the male silverbacks leads his group. Bonobos live in smaller groups than chimpanzees, but their society is led by females instead of males. Orangutans tend to live on their own, although females and their young spend a lot of time together while the youngster is growing up. Gibbons have a completely different social system from that of the other apes—they live in family groups of a mother, father, and their young.

▲ GENTLE GIANTS

Life in a gorilla group is mostly peaceful and friendly, and there is seldom serious fighting within the group. The silverback can stop most quarrels by strutting and glaring at the troublemakers. He is the group's leader, deciding where it will travel and when it will settle down.

Did you know? A silverback male is prepared to die to defend his group.

bonobos
(Pan paniscus)

▼ SOCIABLE SOCIETY

Bonobos are very sociable creatures. Most of the time they live in large, loose groups, called communities, which are split up into smaller groups of 15 or less when they forage for food.

juvenile male   male silverback leader

adult female   young gorilla

◄ HAPPY FAMILIES

Gorillas like to live in extended family groups, usually with between five and 30 members. A gorilla without a group will do its best to join one or start a new one. Each group is controlled and defended by a large adult silverback male.

▲ TREETOP FAMILIES

Gibbons are the only apes that live in pairs and mate for life. They may have two or three young with them, since they do not leave their parents until they are six or seven years old. The gap between births is two-and-a-half to three years.

LONE ORANG ►

Orangutans spend most of their time alone. One reason for this may be that they need to eat a lot of fruit every day. If lots of orangutans lived together, they would not be able to find enough fruit to eat. Even when they do meet, they often ignore each other.

GIRL POWER ►

Females form the backbone of a bonobo group. Adult female bonobos form strong friendships, which are reinforced by grooming and hugging each other. This group of female bonobos have been raised in captivity. Boredom in captivity leads some apes to pluck out their hair.

bonobos
(*Pan paniscus*)

Communication

▼ GIBBON DUET
Many pairs of adult gibbons sing to warn other gibbons to stay out of their territories. The duet may also help the pair to stay together. Singing gibbons fill the forest with a chorus of noisy whoops, hoots, and calls.

Although apes cannot speak, they communicate with a variety of sounds, facial expressions, and gestures. Scientists have even learned some of this ape-speak in order to reassure the apes they are studying, and avoid frightening the animals away. Orangutans and gibbons both call loudly to stake their claim to their territory, just as we would put up a fence and a "keep out" sign around our property. In chimp and gorilla societies, body positions and gestures show which animals are the most important, or dominant, and which are the least important, or submissive. Chimps and gorillas also communicate through a variety of sounds, especially chimps, who can be very noisy apes.

siamang gibbon
(Hylobates syndactylus)

▲ MAKING FACES
Chimpanzees have a variety of different expressions for communication. A wide, open, and relaxed mouth is a play face used to start, or during, a game. An angry chimp clenches his lips shut.

◀ A GAME OF BLUFF

Rising on his back legs, a male silverback gorilla slaps his cupped hands rapidly against his chest, making a "pat-pat-pat" sound. Then he charges forward, tearing up plants and slapping the ground. This display is really a bluff to scare away rivals. Gorillas hardly ever fight, and a male usually stops his charge at the last minute.

▲ GORILLA-SPEAK

Researchers observing gorillas in the wild have learned to make the same sounds and gestures as the gorillas. A content gorilla makes a rumbling, burping sound. A sharp, pig-grunt noise means that the gorilla is annoyed.

◀ KEEP OUT!

Fully grown male orangutans usually keep to their own area of forest—up to six square miles. This is called their home range. Every day, a male roars loudly to warn other orangutans to stay away. This long call lasts for about two minutes. By calling, males avoid meetings that might end in a fight.

TOP CHIMP ▶

The dominant chimpanzee in a group shows off occasionally by charging around, screaming and throwing branches. He also hunches his shoulders and makes his hair stand on end.

▼ LOW RANK

To avoid fighting with important chimps, low-ranking chimps behave in a certain way. They flatten their hair, crouch down or bob up and down, and back toward the more important chimp, while they pant-grunt.

Focus on

All the chimpanzees in a community know each other well. Mothers have a very strong bond with their young, and many chimps who are not related form close friendships, especially males. Dominant males form the stable core of a chimpanzee group, and they will attack and even kill males from other communities. Female chimps may emigrate to a neighboring community. Members of a community meet, spend time together, and then separate throughout the day. In chimp society there is a hierarchy of importance, which is maintained by powerful males. The chimps jostle for position, constantly checking where they stand with each other and challenging their leaders.

YOU GROOM MY BACK

One of the most important activities in a chimpanzee group is grooming. It helps to keep the group together by allowing the chimps to strengthen friendships and patch up quarrels. High-ranking chimps are often groomed by low-ranking ones. It takes a young chimp about two years to learn how to groom properly.

MOTHERS AND BABIES

Rank is not inherited in chimpanzee society, so a young chimp with a high-ranking mother will not necessarily be important itself. But high-ranking mothers are more secure and confident, showing by their behavior how to become a high-ranking chimp. Female chimps become more important in a group as they get older and have more young.

the Chimp Group

GANG WARFARE

A dominant male chimp often makes friends with two or three others, who spend their time with him and back him up in fights. Powerful supporters enable a chimp to become a leader.

PLAYTIME

As young chimpanzees play, they get to know how to mix with the other chimps in a group. They learn how to greet others and which individuals are the most important.

FRIENDSHIP

To show their affection for one another, chimps hug, kiss, and pat each other on the back. Since males spend much more time together than females, this friendly contact is more common between males, although females make special friendships, too.

NOISY CHIMPS

Chimpanzees make over 30 different sounds. When they are content, they make soft "hooing" noises, when they discover food, they hoot, and they scream when they are excited.

Defense

The great apes are too big to be killed and eaten by most animals. Sometimes a tiger, leopard, snake, or crocodile does succeed in catching an ape, although they probably pick on the old, the young, and the sick. Apes can also be injured or even killed in battles with members of their own species. But their main enemy is people, who destroy their habitat, kill them for meat, or capture them as pets or for medical research. Living in a group is a good defense, since members can warn each other of danger and help to defend each other. Apes that live in smaller groups or on their own, such as gibbons and orangutans, can escape danger by living high in the trees.

▲ **SILVER PROTECTION**
If a leopard or a similar predator threatens a group of gorillas, the silverback leader puts himself between his family and the danger. The females and youngsters in the group huddle together and rely on the silverback to drive away the intruder.

◄ **FRIEND OR FOE?**
This frightened chimpanzee is seeking reassurance by holding out her hand. When they are faced with human predators, chimps usually keep quiet and still, or slip away into the bush, but they will attack leopards with long branches and big stones. A chimp's sharp teeth can also inflict a nasty bite.

◀ HUNTED
Leopards are clever hunters, and especially dangerous because they hunt at night. Their spotted coats camouflage them well, and they are excellent tree climbers. Leopards are very agile in trees, so they can spring on apes from overhead.

leopard
(Panthera pardus)

▲ ILLEGAL KILLERS
Apes are protected by law, but poachers (illegal hunters) break the rules because they hope to make money. Here, a pair of gorillas were shot so that their infant could be captured and sold.

Killer Orangutan
In 1841, the American writer, Edgar Allen Poe, published his story The Murders in the Rue Morgue. *In a mysterious and macabre tale, Poe describes how an orangutan escapes from its cage and finds shelter in the home of Madame L'Espanaye and her daughter. Terrified by the two women's cries of fear, the orangutan seizes a razor and cuts their throats.*

▲ CONFUSING GRIN
This chimpanzee may look as if it is smiling, but in fact it is showing its teeth and gums in a fear grin. Chimps make this sort of face when they are frightened or nervous.

Courtship

▲ **ORANGUTAN COURTING**
These young orangutans are practicing their courtship behavior for when they grow up. Courtship in orangutans can last for less than an hour —or it can take many weeks.

Ape courtship involves choosing, attracting, and mating with a partner. Apes breed at any time of year and have various courtship patterns, using sounds, scents, and displays to attract a mate. Chimps and bonobos use mating as a form of communication within their groups. It helps to relieve tension and keep the group together. Females in season accept many different mates, and they mate quickly and often. Mating is less frequent in gorillas and gibbons. They mate mainly to reproduce, but the act lasts somewhat longer. Usually, one male gorilla mates with all the females in his group. Male gibbons usually have just one mate, but some do father other infants. Orangutans pair mainly for courtship and mating, but Sumatran orangutans may stay together for two or three weeks so that the male can protect the pregnant female. Mating lasts much longer and is more varied in orangutans than in other apes.

◀ **IN THE PINK**
When a female chimpanzee is ready to mate, she develops a pinkish swelling on her rear end that sticks out like a pink balloon full of water. This happens every four weeks or so. The female's pink bottom attracts the attention of every nearby male chimp.

chimpanzee
(*Pan troglodytes*)

▲ GIBBON PAIRS

Young male gibbons often sing to attract a female, but they also wander away from their parents in search of a mate. Once a male gibbon finds a mate, he stays with her for life. One of the most characteristic sounds of the Asian forests are the loud, spectacular calls of dueting gibbons echoing through the trees.

▲ PRETEND PLAY

These young gorillas are practicing their fighting skills as they play together. When they grow up and lead their own group, these skills will help them to protect a secure area for the group to live in. Then they will be able to court and mate with the females in their group.

▲ GORILLA MATES

The weather and food supply in a gorilla's habitat are similar all year round, so gorillas mate and give birth at any time of year. Females may ask a male to mate by backing up to the male with their rear end in the air and their elbows on the ground.

▲ HANGING HAIR

Male Sumatran orangutans sometimes display their beautiful orange hair to females by hanging down from branches. This helps a female to decide if he has the strength to protect her from other males.

Focus on

Bonobos live a very peaceful lifestyle and are affectionate and gentle apes. They seem to have adopted a "make love not war" attitude to life. Sexual behavior is an important part of their everyday life, even when they are youngsters. It is used not only for reproduction and having babies, but also as a way of getting along with other group members. Females mate at any time, and with lots of different males, which helps to calm the group down and avoid conflict. Both male and female bonobos also carry out sexually related behavior with others of the same gender. These activities help to constantly reassure the bonobos and keep the group close together.

MALE ROLES

Bonobo males have less status than females, so they do not dominate their groups. Unlike male chimps, male bonobos do not form strong friendships. Instead, they remain close to their mother.

FEMALE IMPORTANCE

The females form the backbone of bonobo groups. Female bonobos may use mating as a way of persuading males to give them food. Low-ranking females seem to mate more than high-ranking ones. This may help them to cope with their less important status in the group, and make the group in general more peaceful.

Bonobos

MATING AD

Their pink bottoms make it very obvious when female bonobos are ready to mate. These mating ads last much longer for bonobos than for chimpanzees.

TENDER TOUCH

Bonobos often touch each other, mate, or groom each other to calm themselves down at a time of excitement or tension. They travel in smaller groups than chimpanzees. Often, a male, a female, and the female's offspring will form a group. Bonobo groups also do not change as much as chimpanzee groups.

BRIEF MATING

Mating for bonobos is a low-key affair, and at least a quarter of all bonobo matings are started by the female. The act of mating lasts only about 15 seconds.

FACE-TO-FACE

Bonobos are unusual among the apes in that they sometimes mate face-to-face, although gorillas, orangutans, and gibbons occasionally do this, too. Mating can be used as a greeting or take place at times of great excitement, such as when a supply of a favorite food has been found.

Birth and Babies

▲ **NEWBORN GORILLA**

This one-day-old gorilla is tiny and helpless. Its wrinkled face is a pinkish color, its big ears stick out, and it has very little hair. Soon after birth, the baby's brown eyes open and peer curiously at its surroundings. Despite its long, skinny arms and legs, the baby gorilla is quite strong.

Like humans, apes usually have one baby at a time and spend many years taking care of their young. With chimps, bonobos, gorillas, and orangutans, the baby develops for about eight or nine months inside its mother before it is born. Baby gibbons are born after a development of only seven or eight months. Baby apes are much smaller than human babies and weigh only about half as much. This means it is much easier for a mother ape to give birth than for a human mother. Both the labor and the birth are fairly fast and easy. Newborn apes are helpless, but they have a very strong grip to cling to their mother's hair. She feeds them on her milk and carries them for four or five years, as they gradually grow up and become independent.

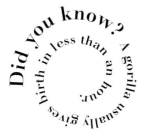
Did you know? A gorilla usually gives birth in less than an hour.

◄ **MILK BAR**

A newborn baby gorilla depends on its mother's milk for nourishment. After six to eight months, it gradually begins to try different kinds of plant food, but it will continue to drink its mother's milk for at least two years.

PIGGYBACK ►

Riding piggyback on its mother's broad back, a baby gorilla watches the other gorillas and looks around its habitat as the group travels from place to place. This is the safest place for the young gorilla until it is strong enough to walk by itself. A young gorilla cannot do this until it is at least two-and-a-half or three years old.

▲ HITCHING A RIDE

Very young baby chimps are carried underneath their mother, clinging onto her fur with their tiny fists. By the age of five or six months, a baby chimp starts to ride on its mother's back. It is alert, looking around and touching things.

◄ TREETOP BABIES

Baby gibbons depend on their mothers for warmth and milk. Gibbon fathers groom their babies and play with them. Siamang gibbon fathers take care of their youngsters during the day.

▲ CHIMP CHILDHOOD

The bond between a mother chimpanzee and her baby is strong, and lasts throughout their lives. A young chimp is completely dependent on its mother for the first five years of its life, and stays where its mother can see or hear it.

Focus on Young

MOTHER LOVE

There is a very strong bond between a mother orangutan and her baby. When she is not moving through the trees or feeding, the mother may groom her baby or suckle it, but she doesn't often play with it. A baby orangutan may scream and throw a tantrum to get its mother's attention.

A young orangutan grows up in a world almost completely filled with its mother, and for the first year of its life, it is totally dependent on her. Following her baby's birth, a mother orangutan becomes even more shy than usual. She tries to avoid other animals in order to protect her baby. The solitary life of a young orangutan is very different from that of a young chimp, bonobo, or gorilla, since they have other youngsters to play with and other adults to help take care of them. A young orangutan stays with its mother for seven to nine years, learning what to eat, where to find food, how to climb and swing through the trees safely, and how to make a nest to sleep in.

MOTHER'S MILK

For the first year of its life, a baby orangutan drinks its mother's milk and clings to her chest or back. After a year, it starts to eat solid food, but it continues to suck for another three to five years. Like most baby mammals, orangutans like to take their mother's milk for as long as possible.

Orang-utans

NEST BUILDING

Baby orangutans share their mother's nest at night. During their second year, they start to experiment with making their own nests.

PLAYTIME

Although they are usually solitary, on the rare occasions young orangutans meet, they wrestle and play together. They may get so carried away that they do not notice when their mother leaves. Then they have to hurry after her, screaming angrily as they go.

SOLID FOOD

To start her baby on solid food, a mother orangutan partly chews up pieces of food and then presses them into the baby's mouth. Young orangutans eagerly take the solid food.

A NEW BABY

When an orangutan is between five and eight years old, its mother may give birth again. The new baby takes the mother's attention, and the young orangutan becomes more independent. It may stay with its mother for a year or more after a new baby is born.

Growing Up

Apes spend a long time growing up. In addition to learning how to move, feed, and defend themselves, they have to know how to behave with others like themselves. This is especially important for chimpanzees and gorillas, because they live in large groups. Young apes do not become independent of their mothers until they are about eight years old. Female orangutans and gorillas may have babies at about 10 years old, but chimps do not have babies until they are about 14 years old. Male gorillas and orangutans mature later than females, at about 15 years old. When they are grown up, orangutans and gibbons leave their parents to start a life of their own. Most gorillas and female chimps also leave the group they were born into.

orangutans
(Pongo pygmaeus)

▲ **MOTHER AND BABY**
Female orangutans spend most of their adult lives caring for their offspring. An orangutan may have only four young in her lifetime.

▲ **APE EXPLORER**
Chimpanzees love to explore, moving farther away from their mothers as they test their climbing skills. At the first sign of danger, they run back to their mother.

▲ **SPEEDY GORILLAS**

Young gorillas develop through the same stages of movement as human babies, only much faster. They can crawl at nine weeks old and walk between five and eight months—a stage when most human babies haven't started to crawl.

◄ **PLAYING THE GAME**

The little chimps have a lot of free time, which they spend at play. Young females spend much of their time playing with the babies in their group. By playing, the chimps learn the rules of chimpanzee society.

chimpanzee
(*Pan troglodytes*)

Did you know? Young gorillas have a white tail tuft to help their mothers find them.

▲ **FOOD FROM MOTHER**

A chimpanzee watches its mother and other chimps to find out what is good to eat. Young chimps chew the other end of whatever food their mother is eating.

▶ **AT PLAY**

Young gorillas wrestle, chase, play-fight, and climb and slide all over the adults. This helps them to test their strength, build up their muscles, and learn how to get along with other gorillas.

Orphan Apes

Sometimes, mother apes are killed by disease, or they die of old age or natural causes, leaving their babies as orphans. Poachers may also kill mothers for meat or to capture their babies. In a zoo, a mother ape may not be able to take care of her baby. All these orphans find life very difficult. They no longer have the comfort of being with their mother and feeling safe under her protection. They cannot watch their mother to learn what to eat and how to behave. People have tried to care for these orphan apes, teaching them how to survive in the wild and releasing them when they can take care of themselves. It takes time for orphans to adapt to life in the wild. They cannot survive if they must compete with wild apes. Many orphan apes are cared for in special sanctuaries, where they have more freedom than in a zoo.

▲ GORILLA ORPHANAGE

The Congolese conservationist, Dr. Ndinga Assitou, holds an orphan gorilla at the Brazzaville Gorilla Orphanage. Sick and wounded little gorillas that have been confiscated from poachers and illegal traders recover and grow up at this orphanage before being returned to the wild.

BOTTLED MILK ▶

The milk of a mother ape contains a balanced mixture of food to help babies grow healthy and strong. Orphan apes are fed on powdered milk, which they drink from bottles. This is not as good for them as their mother's milk, nor do they get the comfort of being held close to their mother's body while they feed.

▲ A NEW LIFE

Baby orangutans were popular as pets in Asia, and poachers still shoot mothers to sell their babies as pets. However, it is illegal to own a pet orangutan. Some of these orphans are taken away from their owners and sent to special centers, where they can be cared for and prepared for a possible life in the wild.

▲ LONELY CHIMP

Baby chimps are very close to their mothers. This emotional bond is so strong that when a mother dies, her infant often dies too. Wild orphans have a better chance of survival if they are cared for by sisters and brothers.

western lowland gorilla
(Gorilla gorilla gorilla)

◄ ZOO APES

Zoos try to leave young apes with their mothers. However, if the mother does not know how to take care of her infant, or if it is sickly, then a keeper has to care for it. Apes that have grown up with keepers, instead of their mothers, tend to behave differently.

▲ HUMAN APES

When apes have lived with humans for a long time, it is difficult for them to get along with other apes of their species. They behave in a different way from wild apes, and they are dependent on people for food. They can only be released back into the wild if a suitably safe habitat can be found, and food provided.

49

Ape Ancestors

The first apes appeared on Earth some 20 million years ago, but their early evolution is difficult to trace accurately, because few of their fossils (preserved remains) have been discovered. Early apes were heavier than monkeys, swinging underneath branches and using their powerful arms for support. Some of these early apes died out, leaving just six groups to evolve through to the present day. Scientific tests suggest that chimpanzees and humans separated from six to eight million years ago, and then began to develop in their own ways. Gorillas branched out earlier, possibly six to nine million years ago, orangutans 12 to 16 million years ago, and gibbons 20 million years ago. However, there is debate about these dates.

▲ HANDY MAN

This is a model of *Homo habilis*, or handy man, an early human named after its ability to make simple stone tools. *Homo habilis* lived about two million years ago in Africa and was four feet tall. Although their brains were only half the size of modern humans, they could probably speak.

FOSSIL APES ▼

Apes probably evolved from a group called *Aegyptopithecus* (Egyptian ape), which lived in North Africa some 30 million years ago. Other fossil apes include *Dryopithecus* or woodland ape (about 18 million years ago), *Ramapithecus* (eight-fifteen million years ago), and *Gigantopithecus* (six–nine million years ago). The *Gigantopithecus* apes died out, but *Dryopithecus* and *Ramapithecus* evolved into modern apes, including humans.

Aegyptopithecus

Dryopithecus

Gigantopithecus

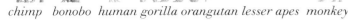
chimp   bonobo   human gorilla orangutan lesser apes   monkey

Did you know? *Apes were more common than monkeys 20 million years ago. Today, the opposite is true.*

0

5

10

15

20

25

30

35

Millions of years ago

◄ FAMILY TREE

There is a lot of debate about the evolution of the apes. This is just one family tree showing possible dates and routes taken by the different apes as they evolved over 20 million years. The human and ape lines of evolution may have separated about five to seven million years ago. Monkeys evolved earlier than apes, about 30 million years ago.

◄ APE THEORY

In 1871, Charles Darwin published a book called *The Descent of Man*, in which he suggested that humans had evolved from apelike ancestors. Many people were shocked by this idea and made fun of Darwin in cartoons such as this one. What Darwin meant was that people and apes evolved along separate lines from earlier, apelike animals.

▼ A COMMON ANCESTOR?

Some scientists have suggested that a small, tree-climbing animal, similar to modern tree shrews, may have been the ancestor of all primates, such as lemurs, monkeys, apes, and humans. However, recent evidence suggests that they might not be as closely related.

Treeshrew *(Tupaia lyonogale tana)*

▲ LEAPING LEGS

A bush baby's back legs can be twice as long as its body. These long legs allow a bush baby to make huge leaps through the rain forest branches. Its large, forward-seeing eyes help it to judge the spaces between branches so that it lands safely.

Primitive Primates

Lemurs, bush babies, lorises, pottos, and tarsiers are all known as primitive primates or prosimians, meaning premonkeys. The other main group of primates—sometimes called the higher primates—includes marmosets and tamarins, monkeys, apes, and humans. Prosimians are different from monkeys, apes, and humans, because they have smaller brains and a much better sense of smell. They also tend to have longer, doglike snouts, and monkeys (except for baboons), apes, and humans have more rounded heads. One of the most distinctive groups of prosimians is the lemurs of Madagascar. The name lemur means ghost and refers to their mysterious life in the trees. Early primates may have looked like modern lemurs and followed a similar lifestyle.

STRIPED TAILS ▶

Ring-tailed lemurs live in groups with up to 30 members. The striped tail is longer than the total length of the head and body. It is used for signaling messages to other lemurs, and can also be rubbed with a scent to send smelly messages. The sense of smell is more important for lemurs than for apes.

ring-tailed lemurs
(Lemur catta)

FINGER FOOD ▶

The most extraordinary part of an aye-aye's body is its long, skinny middle finger. It uses this to extract wood-boring insects from tree trunks, and scoop the insides out of hard-shelled fruits. Unlike other primates, the aye-aye has claws on the ends of its fingers and most toes.

◀ STILL AS STONE

The potto lives among thick rain forest vegetation and moves so slowly and carefully that it is very hard to see. At the slightest sign of danger, the potto freezes completely. It can stay like this for hours. Its grasping feet and hands give it a strong grip on branches.

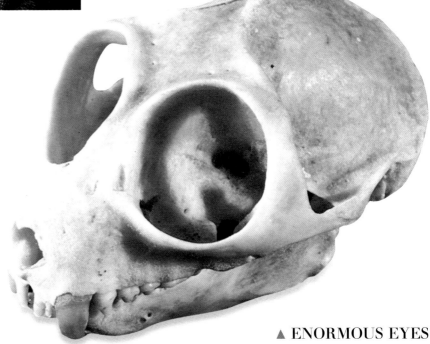

▲ TWIN TAXI

This silvery marmoset is the father of the two babies on his back. Father marmosets are very involved in bringing up babies—which is hard work because marmosets usually have twins.

▲ ENORMOUS EYES

The most obvious feature of a loris's skull is its huge eye sockets, which are protected by a thick, bony ridge. A loris is active at night and needs its huge eyes to help it see in the dark. Lorises also have a well-developed sense of smell, and a face covered with hair.

Monkeys

From the tiny pygmy marmoset to the huge mandrill, the 130 species of monkey alive today are a varied and successful group. Unlike apes, most have tails, but they are similar in many other ways, being playful, inquisitive, and clever. They tend to live in groups, and many are very good at learning things. They can also see in depth and in color. Modern monkeys are split into two groups. New World monkeys from the Americas have wide, splayed nostrils set far apart, no sitting pads, and many have a prehensile tail for holding onto branches. Old World monkeys from Africa and Asia have close-set nostrils that face downward, sitting pads and a nonprehensile tail. Despite the differences, the groups are still related.

▲ NOISY MONKEYS

Howler monkeys make some of the loudest calls in the animal world. The howl is made by passing air through a space inside a large bone in the throat. Howlers live in troops in the South American rain forest. Their loud howls warn other troops to keep out of their territory, so that they can avoid fights over food and other resources.

Brown capuchin
(Cebus apella)

◄ CLEVER CAPUCHINS
Capuchin monkeys are sometimes called South American chimps because of the way they use tools, such as rocks and branches, to crack open nuts and shells.

▲ OLD WORLD MONKEYS

The monkeys of Asia and Africa are called Old World monkeys. They include monkeys such as baboons (above), guenons, macaques, colobus, and leaf monkeys. You can see the sitting pads on the baboon on the left.

▲ HOT BATH

Japanese macaques live in the mountains of Honshu, where it gets very cold in the winter. One group takes baths in hot volcanic springs, which helps them to keep warm even when they are surrounded by snow.

◄ TAILS

Tails come in all shapes and sizes. With monkeys from Central and South America, such as this black spider monkey, the prehensile tail grips so well that it works like an extra hand. Tree-living monkeys use their tails for balance.

black spider monkey
(*Ateles paniscus*)

Did you know? The howls of the red howler monkey can be heard up to 2 mi. away.

Monkey God
The Ancient Egyptian god Thoth sometimes had the head of a hamadryas baboon. Thoth was regarded as a god of learning, science, the arts, and writing. The pharaoh's royal scribes, such as the one in this statue, were believed to be inspired by the baboon-headed god.

Working Primates

People have often used monkeys and apes for entertainment, to help them complete certain tasks, or for scientific experiments. Sometimes they are well cared for, but often they are kept in very bad conditions and do not live long. They may even die on the journey from their natural habitat, especially if they are transported in small, cramped containers with no food or water. Even when they do survive, captured apes or monkeys live a very artificial life, away from their natural homes and their friends and families. Some of them may suffer a lot of pain during scientific experiments. In an ideal world, we would stop using apes or monkeys for our own purposes. We should certainly prevent the use of such intelligent creatures simply as playthings and conversation pieces.

▲ APE ADS
Chimpanzees are sometimes dressed up in human clothes and used in commercials. Although some people can make a lot of money, others believe it is wrong to use apes in this way.

◄ TRIED AND TRUE
Many chimps have been used for medical research, because they are so similar to humans. Gorillas and orangutans are too big to keep and handle easily. In the 1960s and 1970s, chimps were forced to smoke cigarettes to test for lung diseases. They were also used for brain experiments. Today, such harmful and inhuman experiments are less common, but some are still tested with diseases in some countries.

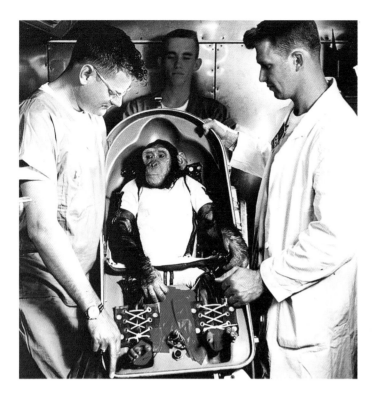

▲ SPACE APE

In 1961, a chimp was the first live creature to be sent into space by the United States. He was monitored throughout the flight by cameras. This flight paved the way for the first human space voyages, but we can only guess at how the chimp felt about such a terrifying experience.

▲ HELPING HAND

In Thailand, pig-tailed macaques are trained to collect coconuts for their owners in return for food rewards. The macaques are much better than people at climbing trees.

◀ BEACH CHIMPS

Visitors to popular beaches in the Mediterranean may have their picture taken with a young chimpanzee. They do not realize that many of these chimps are illegal and ill-treated by their owners. Most die of neglect within a year or so. The use of beach chimps has been banned in many areas, but not wiped out completely.

▲ MOVIE STAR

A female orangutan starred alongside Clint Eastwood in the movie *Every Which Way But Loose* (1978) and in the sequel *Any Which Way You Can*. The plot featured the travels of a prize fighter and an orangutan named Clyde.

Apes in Danger

Apes live in a steadily shrinking habitat. Their forest and woodland homes have been gradually replaced by farms, grazing lands, and villages. Vast areas of rain forest have been flooded by the water held back by dams, and other areas have been dug up by mining companies looking for precious minerals and metals. Even when apes live in protected areas, they are still illegally hunted for their meat or body parts, or captured to be sold as pets or for medical research. In times of war, apes are further threatened by land mines and the movement of large numbers of refugees into their habitat. People can also transfer diseases to apes, often without realizing that they have done so.

▲ POACHING

This is some of the equipment used by poachers to kill apes and antelopes illegally in protected areas, such as national parks. Wire traps concealed in the brush can prove deadly to apes trapped in their tight grip. Traditional hunting weapons, such as spears and arrows, may also be used.

Did you know? There are just 630 mountain gorillas in the world.

APE BODIES ▶

Ape body parts are sometimes sold as grisly souvenirs. These gorilla skulls are for sale on a traditional medicine stall in Africa, where they are used as fetishes (a type of good luck charm). There would be no reason for poachers to kill apes if people were not prepared to buy their body parts. Gorillas are also killed for meat. Some of it feeds workers cutting down the forests. The rest is sold in city markets.

▲ FOREST DESTRUCTION

The greatest danger to all apes and monkeys is the destruction of their habitat, especially the rain forests. An area of rain forest the size of four football fields disappears every minute. Rain forests are destroyed for their valuable timber, or to make way for cattle ranches or plantations of cash crops.

▲ THREAT OF WAR

In the mid-1990s, civil war and genocide in Rwanda led thousands of people to raid the national park of the mountain gorillas for firewood and food.

▲ DISEASES

Since apes are so similar to us, they suffer from many of the same diseases. For example, apes can catch malaria, carried by mosquitoes.

FOREST FIRES ▶

In the late 1990s, forest fires raged across Borneo and Sumatra, killing many orangutans, destroying their habitat, and causing breathing problems for the survivors.

▲ GORILLAS IN THE MIST
Dian Fossey wrote about her work with mountain gorillas in *Gorillas in the Mist*, later made into a film starring Sigourney Weaver (above). The film raised awareness of the gorilla's plight.

▼ HABITAT ZOOS
Some good zoos now keep apes in large, tree-filled enclosures, which are as much like their natural habitat as possible. Breeding apes in zoos helps to increase their numbers.

Conservation

Gorillas, orangutans, chimpanzees, and bonobos are now officially recognized as endangered species. Laws have been passed to stop live apes and parts of their bodies from being bought or sold. However, laws can never give total protection to wild animals, especially when people can make a lot of money by breaking the law. To help apes survive in the future, their habitat needs to be protected in national parks or reserves. Apes bred in captivity might one day be released into the wild, but only if suitable natural habitats can be found. Conserving apes takes a lot of time and costs a lot of money. Many of the countries where the apes live have very little money and need help for conservation from richer nations. Apes are more like humans than any other animal. It will be tragic if we cannot find a way to share our future with them.

western lowland gorillas
(Gorilla gorilla gorilla)

▲ TOURIST DOLLARS

Many people pay a lot of money to get close to a wild ape, but this is too close, since the ape could catch a human flu. If tourists are carefully controlled, they provide money to pay for conservation.

▼ POACHING PATROL

These wardens are patrolling the national park where the mountain gorillas live. They are keeping a sharp lookout for armed poachers and their traps. If there is a shoot-out, both the wardens and the poachers may be killed.

◄ CHIMFUNSHI ORPHANAGE

David and Sheila Siddle have converted their farm in Zambia into the Chimfunshi Wildlife Orphanage to take care of rescued chimps from the Congo. The Siddles have walled and fenced off their land, and allow the chimps to climb trees, build nests, and live like wild chimpanzees.

► EDGE OF SURVIVAL

In developing countries where most families grow their own food, there is an increasing need for more land. Forests are cleared right up to the park boundary, as seen in this photograph, which shows the edge of the Virunga National Park in the Congo. If gorillas and elephants wander out searching for food, they are labeled "crop raiders" by local farmers, who are anxious to protect their only source of food or income.

GLOSSARY

ape
An intelligent primate with no tail, a small nose, long arms, and grasping hands and feet, with nails instead of claws. Apes are active in the daytime and have excellent eyesight. (See **great apes, lesser apes**)

blackback
An adolescent male gorilla, aged 8 to 10 years, whose back has not yet turned silver.

bonobo
A great ape that lives in the African rain forests of the Congo. It looks like a chimpanzee and is sometimes called a pygmy chimpanzee.

brachiation
Moving by swinging from one hand to another beneath a branch, as gibbons do.

camouflage
Colors, patterns, or shapes that allow an animal to blend in with its surroundings.

canines
Sharp, pointed teeth next to the incisors at the front of a mammal's jaw. Canines are used for piercing and tearing food, and for defense.

cash crop
Crops that are grown for cash (money) rather than for food.

civil war
A war that is fought between different groups within the same country.

community
A large social group of individuals, such as chimpanzees or humans, who live together.

conservation (of nature)
Protecting living things and helping them to survive.

deciduous forests
Forests made up of trees that lose their leaves in the winter or during a dry season.

digest
To break down food so that it can be absorbed into the body and provide energy.

dominant animal
A "top" animal that the other members of a group allow to lead or to take first place.

endangered species
A species of animal or plant that is likely to die out in the near future.

evolution
The process by which living things change gradually over many generations.

fossils
The preserved remains of living things usually found in the rocks.

great apes
The four largest apes—chimps, bonobos, gorillas, and orangutans. Humans are also classed, by some people, as a great ape.

grooming
The cleaning of an animal's fur, either by itself or by another indiviual. Grooming calms animals down and helps them to make friends and avoid conflict.

habitat
The place where an animal naturally lives.

incisors
The cutting teeth of mammals, which are at the front of the jaw.

labor
The process of giving birth.

lesser apes
The 11 species of gibbon, which are smaller than the great apes and live in trees all the time. They can move by brachiation and do not build nests.

lowland gorillas
The two subspecies of gorilla (western and eastern lowland gorillas) that live in the lowland rain forests of Central Africa.

mammal
An animal with a backbone, fur, or hair that can control its own body temperature (is warm-blooded). Females feed their young on milk made in the mammary glands.

mature animal
A fully developed animal that is able to breed.

molars
The chewing and grinding teeth at the side of a mammal's jaw.

monkey
A clever, playful primate with a tail. They usually have a round face and a small nose. Monkeys are active in the daytime and live in groups. Many of them live in trees.

mountain gorilla
A very endangered subspecies of gorilla, with long hair, which lives in the mountains of the Virunga volcanoes (on the borders of the Congo, Rwanda, and Uganda), and in Uganda's Bwindi-Impenetrable forest.

opposable digit
A thumb or toe that can touch the fingers or toes in a gripping action, allowing objects to be held firmly.

orphan
An animal without any parents.

poaching
Capturing and/or killing animals illegally, usually to sell for commercial gain.

predator
An animal that catches and kills other animals for food.

prehensile tail
A tail that is adapted for grasping and holding.

prey
An animal that is hunted and killed by other animals.

primates
A group of mammals that includes lemurs, bush babies, monkeys, apes, and humans. Primates are intelligent animals that mainly live in trees and have limbs adapted for climbing, swinging, or leaping. They have flexible fingers and toes, and forward-pointing eyes.

prosimians
The group of primates that includes lemurs, bush babies, lorises, pottos, and tarsiers. Prosimians have smaller brains, but a better sense of smell than other primates. They are usually active at night.

pygmy chimpanzee
See **bonobo**.

rain forest
A type of forest that is wet during all seasons.

sagittal crest
A large bony crest on the top of the skull in some primates, especially adult male gorillas.

silverback
An adult male gorilla named after the saddle-shaped area of silver hair on his back.

species
A group of animals that shares similar characteristics and can breed together to produce fertile offspring.

submissive animal
An animal that does not occupy an important position in a group and yields to dominant individuals.

termite
A social insect with biting mouthparts, which lives in hot countries.

territory
An area of land that one or more animals defend against members of the same and other species.

troop
The name given to a group of monkeys.

vocal cords
Two folds of skin in the throats of warm-blooded animals, which vibrate and produce sound when air passes over them.

volcano
A crack in the Earth's crust, through which molten rock and gases from inside the Earth escape onto the surface and solidify. An active volcano is one that can erupt at any time. A dormant or "sleeping" volcano is one that has not erupted for many years.

INDEX

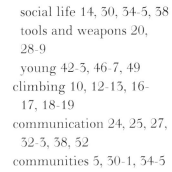

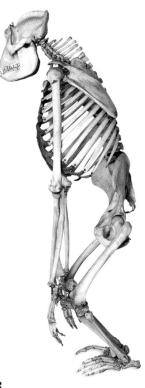